MESOPOTAMIA

by Catherine C. Finan

BEARPORT
PUBLISHING

Minneapolis, Minnesota

Credits:

Title page, 12 top background, 22 top, Sir Austen Henry Layard/Public Domain; 4 top, Best-Backgrounds/Shutterstock; 4 bottom left, 9 top left, Darafsh/Creative Commons; 4 bottom right, Fun Fun Photo/Shutterstock.com; 5 top, Osama alqasab/Creative Commons; 5 top right, 5 bottom left, 15 bottom right, 26 bottom middle, LightField Studios/Shutterstock; 5 middle, Dima Moroz/Shutterstock; 5 bottom, 19 bottom middle, Fred Romero/Creative Commons; 6 top, Acdixon/Creative Commons; 6 left, 9 bottom middle, 11 bottom middle, 18 top middle, 24 bottom, 26 bottom left, 27 figure top left, Albert Kretschmer, painters and costumer to the Royal Court Theatre, Berlin, and Dr. Carl Rohrbach/Public Domain; 6 top right, 11 top middle, 11 bottom, 12 bottom left, 17 bottom, 19 - priest - middle, 23 bottom, 24 top, James Tissot/Public Domain; 7 top, Public Domain; 7 middle, Anthony Huan/Creative Commons; 7 bottom, Iglonghurst/Creative Commons; 7 bottom left, Zur Geschichte der Kostüme/Public Domain; 8 top right, Couperfield/Shutterstock; 8 bottom, Bert van der Spek/Creative Commons; 8 bottom left, Fedor Selivanov/Shutterstock; 8 bottom middle, Brocreative/Shutterstock; 8 bottom right, Kotomiti Okuma/Shutterstock; 9 top, e.backlund/Shutterstock; 9 top right, Viacheslav Lopatin/Shutterstock.com; 9 bottom, Jukka Palm/Shutterstock; 9 bottom, left & right, Design Projects/Shutterstock; 10 top, Maj. Mike Feeney/U.S. military/Public Domain; 10 bottom left, 13 bottom, 16 top left. figure, 22 bottom, Edwin Long/Public Domain; 10 bottom right, fizkes/Shutterstock; 11 top left, Sammy33/Shutterstock; 11 bottom, Radomil, CM/Creative Commons; 11 middle, Lakeview Images/Shutterstock; 12 top middle, Mbzt/Creative Commons; 12 bottom right, Oliver Denker/Shutterstock; 13 top, US. Government photo/Public Domain; 13 bottom middle, Dima Moroz/Shutterstock; 14 top, 15 top, Gtoffoletto/Creative Commons; 14 bottom right, Sammy33/Shutterstock; 15 bottom, Gary Todd/Public Domain; 15 bottom left, Another Believer/Creative Commons; 15 bottom middle, Elena Nichizhenova/Shutterstock; 16 top left, Valentyna Chukhlyebova/Shutterstock; 16 bottom, Acdixon/Creative Commons; 17 top, Poliorketes/Shutterstock; 17 top left, Elnur/Shutterstock; 17 top right, Kletr/Shutterstock; 17 middle, Michael Rosskothen/Shutterstock; 17 upper bottom, us-tas7777777/Shutterstock; 17 bottom, Nina Alizada/Shutterstock; 18 top, tsuneomp/Shutterstock; 18 bottom, Maria Gniloskurenko/Shutterstock; 19 top, 21 bottom right, Myths and legends of Babylonia & Assyria/Public Domain; 19 middle, Elena11/Shutterstock; 19 bottom, vovan/Shutterstock; 19 bottom left, Jastrow/Public Domain; 19 bottom right, insta_photos/Shutterstock; 20 top, Antonio Soletti/Shutterstock; 20 middle, Daderot/Creative Commons; 20 bottom left, 20 bottom right, Eric Isselee/Shutterstock; 20 bottom middle, Rama/Creative Commons; 21 top background, Kirienko Oleg/Shutterstock; 21 bottom of top image, Design Projects/Shutterstock; 21 top right, Public Domain; 21 bottom, David Orcea/Shutterstock; 21 bottom left, Osama Shukir Muhammed Amin FRCP(Glasg)/Creative Commons; 23 top, BabelStone/Creative Commons; 23 middle, Imran Khan Photography/Shutterstock; 23 bottom middle, Roman Samborskyi/Shutterstock; 25 top, Georges Rochegrosse/Public Domain; 25 middle, Tilemahos Efthimiadis/Creative Commons; 25 bottom left, 27 bottom left, Prostock-studio/Shutterstock; 25 bottom middle, Romariolen/Shutterstock; 25 bottom right, Dragon Images/Shutterstock; 26 top left, Sarinra/Shutterstock; 26 top right, Gary Todd/Creative Commons; 26 bottom, Lurin/Shutterstock; 27 top, Lolostock/Shutterstock; 27 bottom, NavinTar/Shutterstock; 27 bottom right, Jeka/Shutterstock; 28 top left, Ben Pirard/Creative Commons; 28 left middle, Marie-Lan Nguyen/Public Domain; 28 left bottom, Zunkir/Creative Commons; 28–29, Austen Photography

President: Jen Jenson
Director of Product Development: Spencer Brinker
Senior Editor: Allison Juda
Associate Editor: Charly Haley
Designer: Colin O'Dea

Developed and produced for Bearport Publishing by BlueAppleWorks Inc.
Managing Editor for BlueAppleWorks: Melissa McClellan
Art Director: T.J. Choleva
Photo Research: Jane Reid

Library of Congress Cataloging-in-Publication Data

Names: Finan, Catherine C., 1972- author.
Title: Mesopotamia / Catherine C Finan.
Description: Minneapolis, Minnesota : Bearport Publishing Company, [2022] |
   Series: X-treme facts: Ancient history | Includes bibliographical
   references and index.
Identifiers: LCCN 2021001082 (print) | LCCN 2021001083 (ebook) | ISBN
   9781636910970 (library binding) | ISBN 9781636911045 (paperback) | ISBN
   9781636911113 (ebook)
Subjects: LCSH: Iraq--Civilization--To 634--Juvenile literature.
Classification: LCC DS70.62 .F56 2022 (print) | LCC DS70.62 (ebook) | DDC
   935--dc23
LC record available at https://lccn.loc.gov/2021001082
LC ebook record available at https://lccn.loc.gov/2021001083

For more information, write to Bearport Publishing, 5357 Penn Avenue South, Minneapolis, MN 55419.
Printed in the United States of America.

Contents

Coming in First 4

It All Started in Sumer 6

They Wrote It First! 8

The Rise of Beautiful Babylonia 10

Hammurabi's Code 12

The Fearsome Assyrians 14

Lots and Lots of Ziggurats 16

Awesome Astrologers 18

Gods Gone Wild 20

At Home in Mesopotamia 22

The Persian Empire 24

Magnificent Mesopotamia 26

Signatory Seals 28

Glossary 30

Read More 31

Learn More Online 31

Index 32

About the Author 32

Coming in First

Are you ready to travel back—way back—to a time many thousands of years ago when most humans had no permanent home? Instead, they wandered around in small groups, constantly searching for food and water.

But wait . . . what's that up ahead? It looks like a village. We've made it to Mesopotamia, the location of the first human civilization *ever*!

Mesopotamia means the land between two rivers. It sat between the Tigris and Euphrates rivers, an area that is now Iraq and other countries.

Fertile Crescent

Caspian Sea

Tigris River

M E S O P O T A M I A

Euphrates River

Mediterranean Sea

SUPERMAN, I WAS MIGHTIER THAN YOU IN MY TIME!

Persian Gulf

Mesopotamia was part of the area known as the Fertile Crescent, named for the rich soil along the rivers that was good for crops.

Mesopotamia gave the world its first hero—Gilgamesh. He was said to be the strongest man in the world!

The world's first large city, Uruk, was in Mesopotamia. About 50,000 people lived there!

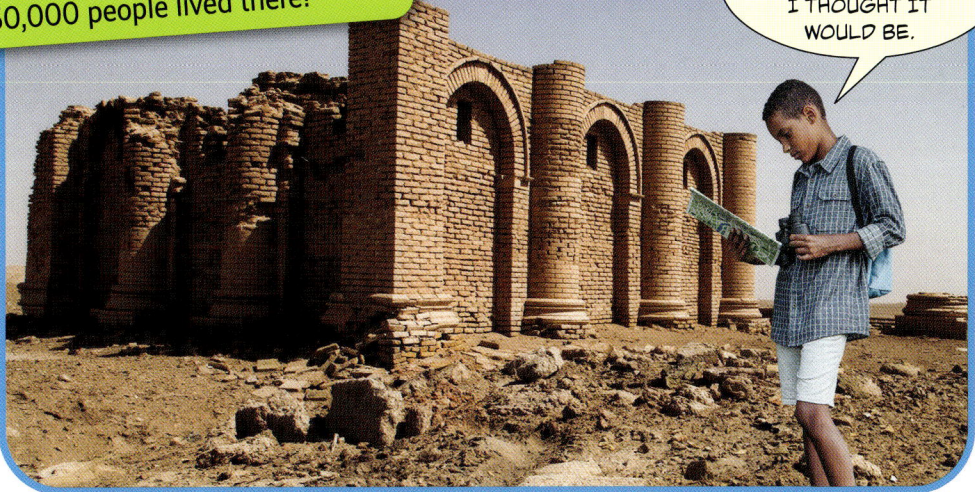

THIS IS URUK, RIGHT? IT'S SMALLER THAN I THOUGHT IT WOULD BE.

Mesopotamia earned the nickname the Cradle of Civilization because it gave birth to the first cities, the first farming, and the first system of writing.

People in Mesopotamia came up with the 60-minute hour.

BIG DEAL! I'VE BEEN WAITING HERE SINCE THE HOUR WAS INVENTED.

WHEN WILL THIS MUSEUM OPEN? I'VE BEEN STANDING HERE FOR AN HOUR!

It All Started in Sumer

So, how did the world's first civilization get its start? Well, it's a *long* story. . . . More than 10,000 years ago, **nomadic** tribes began to settle in northern Mesopotamia. Over thousands of years, the small communities stayed and learned to use water from the Tigris and Euphrates to help grow crops. Gradually, these communities spread south and grew into larger towns. Over time, the first major cities formed in a region called Sumer. And this was just the beginning!

The oldest wheel ever discovered was from Mesopotamia. Wheels were probably first used to make pottery rather than for transportation.

OH, NOTHING . . . I'M JUST TRYING TO REINVENT THE WHEEL.

WHAT ARE YOU FIDDLING WITH OVER THERE, POTTER?

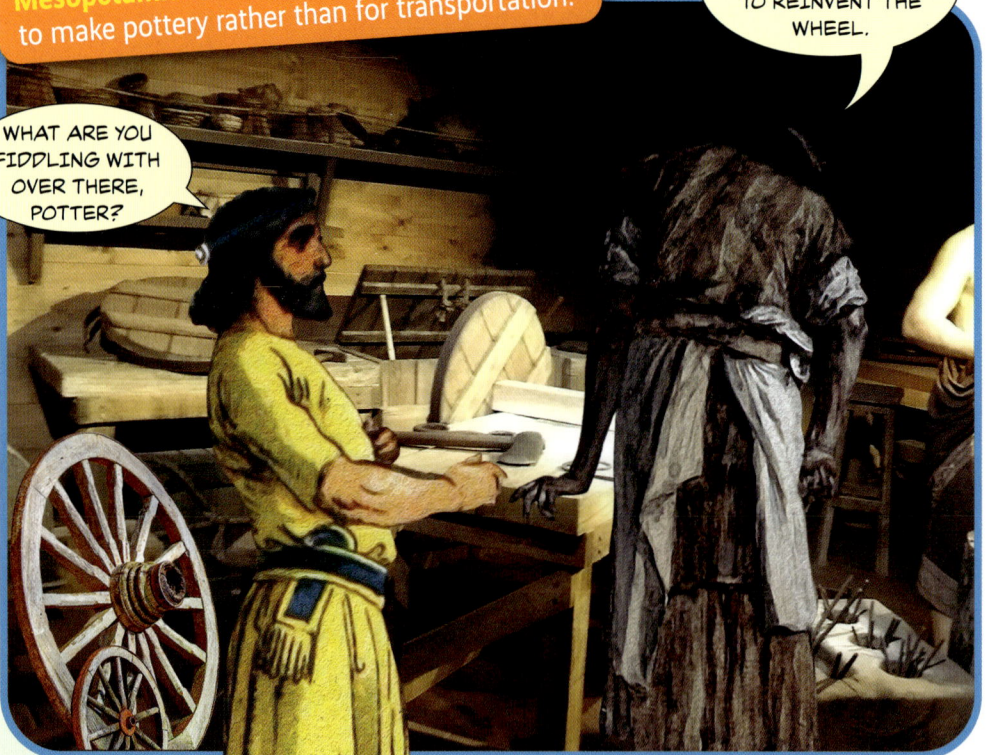

The first sailboat was invented by the Sumerians.

WHERE ARE OUR SAILS?

THERE'S NO WIND TODAY. KEEP ROWING!

The Sumerians may have made the first **chariots**, too.

The Akkadians of northern Mesopotamia conquered the Sumerians around 2,270 BCE. Then, King Sargon of Akkad ruled over all of Mesopotamia.

IS MY ARMY READY FOR BATTLE?

YES, SIR! YOU CAN BEGIN CONQUERING SUMER THIS SUMMER.

Sargon of Akkad built the world's very first **empire** in Mesopotamia and had the world's first permanent army.

They Wrote It First!

The Sumerians didn't just build the world's first cities and invent the wheel—they also wrote about it! They created the world's first system of writing, called cuneiform (kyu-NEE-uh-form). Pictures and characters were pressed into soft clay tablets with **wedge**-shaped sticks. The clay hardened as it dried, leaving a lasting written record. Cuneiform was used mainly for government and business records, but the ancient writing also included stories, poetry, and songs.

COME HERE, KID! I'LL SHOW YOU HOW TO READ THIS.

The word cuneiform means wedge-shaped. Can you guess why?

NO, THANKS! I'VE ALREADY GOT A TON OF HOMEWORK.

Unlike the modern English alphabet with 26 letters, cuneiform used more than 700 different symbols.

Each cuneiform symbol represented a word or sound.

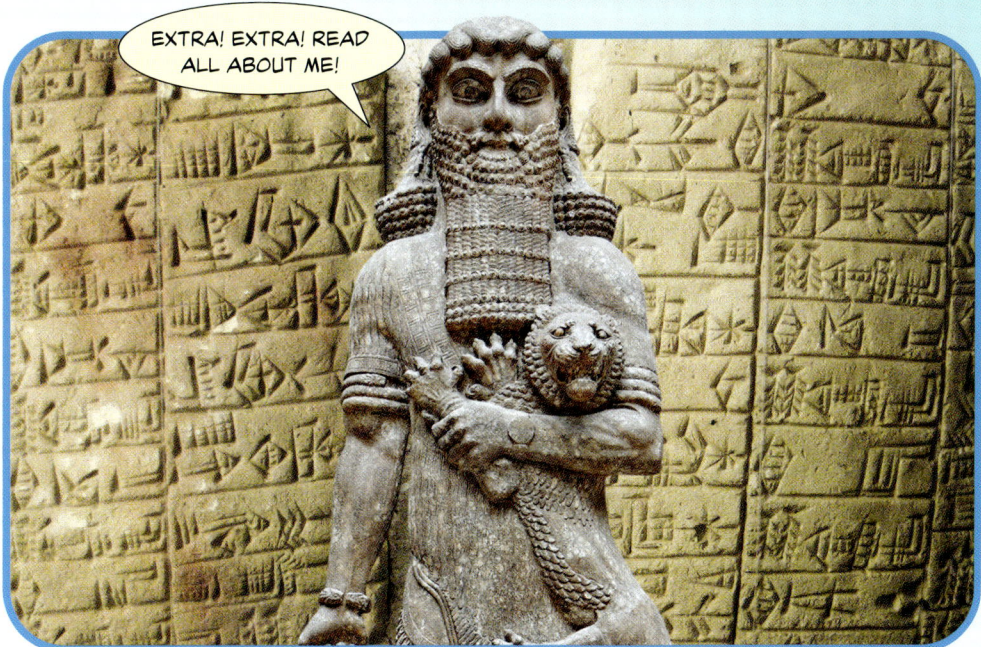

Sumerian tales of the half-human, half-god Gilgamesh are preserved on cuneiform tablets.

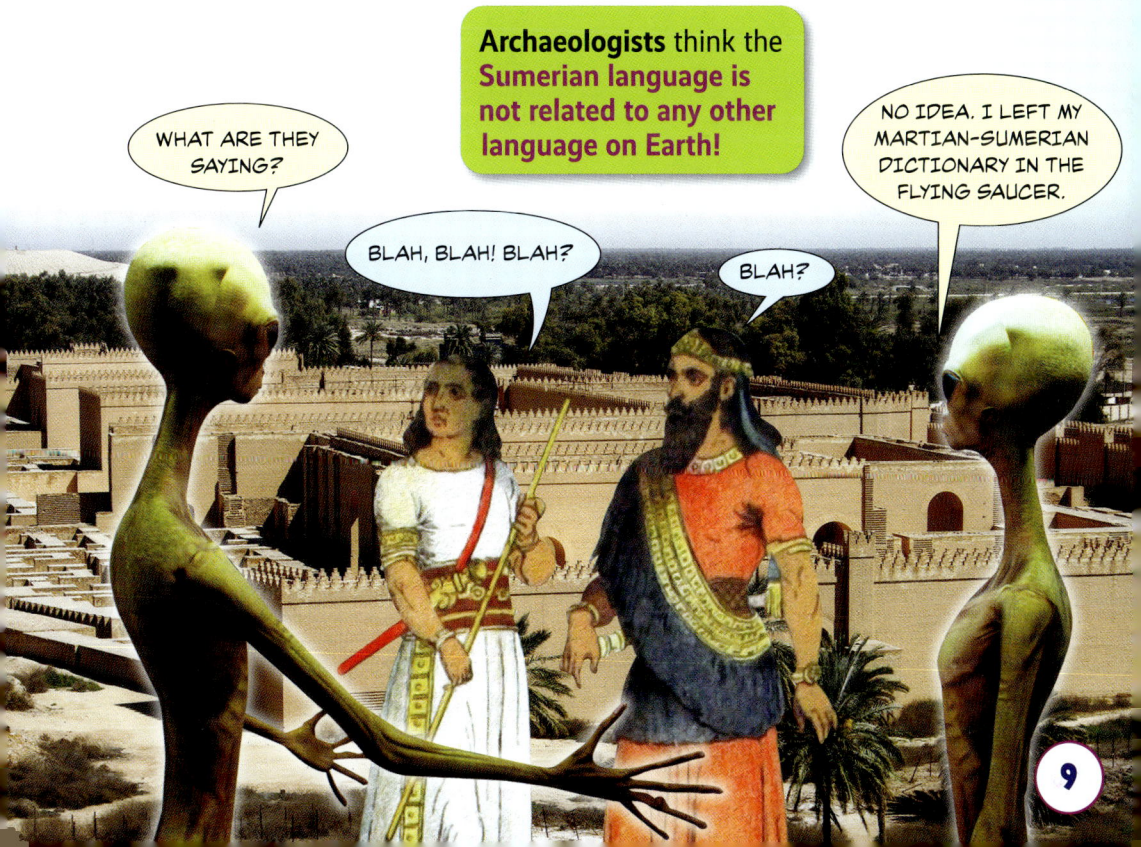

Archaeologists think the Sumerian language is not related to any other language on Earth!

9

The Rise of Beautiful Babylonia

Thanks to the history preserved on cuneiform tablets, we have a glimpse into the drama that unfolded after the Akkadians conquered Sumer. The Akkadians soon lost power, and two new empires quickly rose to take their place—the Assyrians in the north and the Babylonians in the south. Then, under the leadership of King Hammurabi, the Babylonians quickly conquered most of Mesopotamia.

Babylon was the capital city of Babylonia. It became **the world's largest and most powerful city!**

JUST WAIT UNTIL THEY INVENT CARS!

YES! THIS CITY IS TOO CROWDED AND NOISY!

DO YOU HAVE A HEADACHE?

At one time, **200,000 people lived in Babylon.**

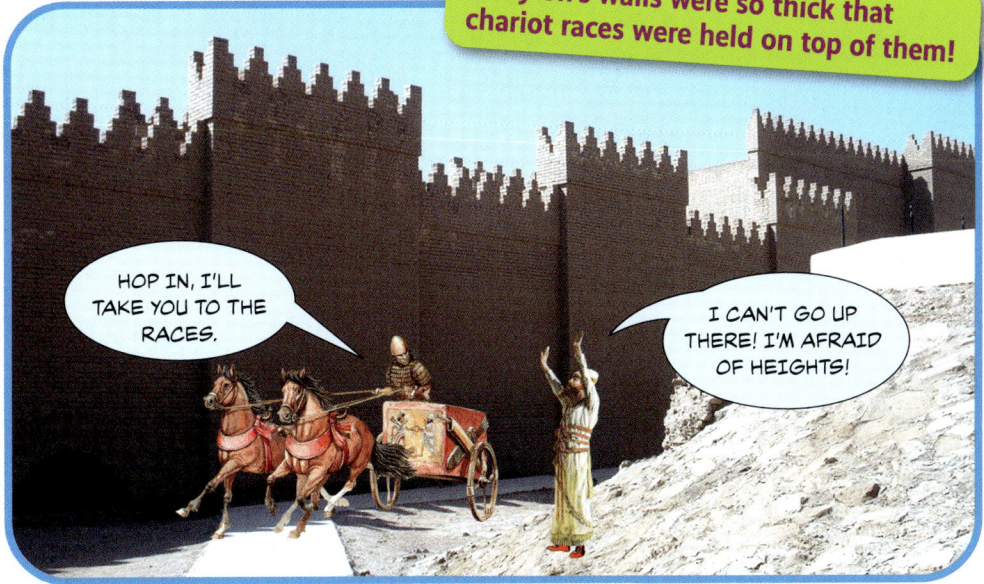

HOP IN, I'LL TAKE YOU TO THE RACES.

I CAN'T GO UP THERE! I'M AFRAID OF HEIGHTS!

Giant walls made of more than 15 million bricks protected the city of Babylon from enemies.

During his life, **Hammurabi** was considered a god!

After Hammurabi's death, his son took over the empire, but it quickly fell apart.

ARE YOU GOING TO GIVE THE EMPIRE TO ME, DAD?

YES, SON. BUT JUST PROMISE ME THAT YOU WON'T SCREW THIS UP!

IS HIS SON A GOD, TOO?

NAH, HE'S NOTHING LIKE HIS FATHER!

11

Hammurabi's Code

Along with making Babylon the most powerful city in the world, King Hammurabi also created one of history's first written codes of law. And he wasn't kidding around! The Code of Hammurabi included a whopping 282 laws, all recorded on a huge slab of stone so everyone could read them. Breaking one of these laws often led to a pretty harsh punishment.

Legends say that Hammurabi received the codes of law from Shamash, **the Babylonian god of justice.**

DID YOU SAY TO WRITE THE CODE ON A BONE?

STONE! I SAID TO WRITE IT IN STONE!

WHAT HAPPENS IF I KICK YOU INSTEAD?

YOU BETTER KEEP YOUR HANDS TO YOURSELF, SON!

According to the code, **if a son hit his father, his hand would be cut off!** Behave . . . or else!

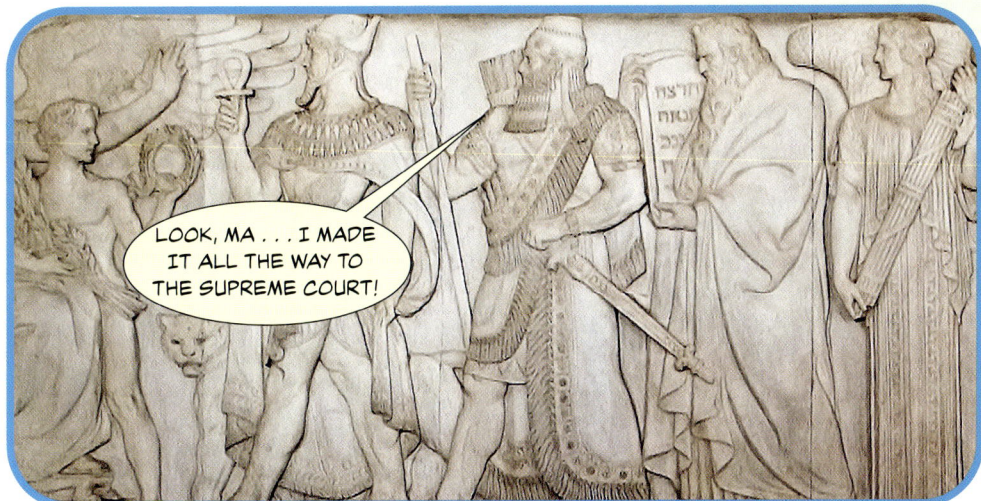

LOOK, MA . . . I MADE IT ALL THE WAY TO THE SUPREME COURT!

Both the U.S. Supreme Court Building and the U.S. Capitol have artwork honoring Hammurabi as one of history's greatest lawmakers.

The saying *an eye for an eye* comes from Hammurabi's Code. If you took out another person's eye, you'd lose your own!

While many punishments were harsh, the code also said that people are innocent until proven guilty.

WHAT DOES IT SAY? I CAN'T READ IT FROM HERE WITH MY ONE EYE.

WOW, HAMMURABI SURE HAS A LOT OF RULES!

Today, you can see the stone carved with the Code of Hammurabi at the Louvre Museum in Paris, France.

13

The Fearsome Assyrians

King Hammurabi's famous Babylonian Empire was matched by another fearsome force in northern Mesopotamia—the Assyrian Empire. The Assyrians conquered others to grow their empire across much of the **Middle East**. The empire was known for its fierce army. Enemies never liked to see them coming!

War was a part of life in the Assyrian Empire. Their warriors were famous for their cruelty.

WELL, MAKING ALL THOSE PEOPLE DIE OF THIRST WASN'T VERY NICE!

I WOULDN'T SAY WE'RE CRUEL, WOULD YOU?

OUR ARMOR WASN'T TOO SHABBY, EITHER!

Sometimes the Assyrians would conquer an enemy city by cutting off its water supply.

The Assyrians' iron weapons were much stronger—and deadlier—than the copper and tin weapons of their enemies.

The Assyrians were master chariot drivers, which gave them an edge in battle.

Assyria's King Ashurbanipal built a huge library to preserve Mesopotamia's treasures. The Code of Hammurabi and the stories of Gilgamesh were kept there.

Ashurbanipal's library held over 30,000 cuneiform tablets. Most of what we know about Mesopotamia comes from his library.

Lots and Lots of Ziggurats

No matter which empire controlled Mesopotamia, some things remained the same, including the **worship** of the gods and the ziggurats devoted to them. From the time of the Sumerians, Mesopotamian cities were built around ziggurats, which were huge temples dedicated to each city's main god. Ziggurats were made from sun-dried mud bricks and were often part of a temple **complex** with other buildings. Each ziggurat had stairs that led to the very top, where priests offered gifts and **sacrifices** to the gods.

Babylon's ziggurat, called Etemenanki, was twice the height of the Statue of Liberty!

WORK HARDER, PEOPLE! BUILD IT NICE AND TALL! I WANT THIS ZIGGURAT TO GET INTO THE RECORD BOOKS!

Etemenanki honored Marduk, ruler of the gods and proud owner of a pet dragon!

WHAT IS THAT UP THERE?

IT'S JUST THE BOSS CHECKING UP ON US!

DO YOU WANT ME TO SCORCH THE LAZY ONES?

Most ziggurats had between two and seven floors.

I'M SO BORED. WHEN ARE YOU GOING TO STOP COUNTING THESE BRICKS?

ARGH! YOU MADE ME LOSE COUNT AGAIN! ONE, TWO, THREE . . .

Ziggurats were usually made using millions of bricks. That's a lot of mud!

People believed that the gods slept at the tops of the ziggurats at night. Slumber party!

Ordinary people were not allowed to climb the stairs of the ziggurats. The priests wanted to keep their rooftop **rituals** a secret!

IT SOUNDS LIKE THEY'RE HAVING A GREAT PARTY UP THERE!

PARTY TIME!

WOO-HOO!

YEAH, THE GODS HAVE ALL THE FUN.

17

Awesome Astrologers

Along with daily worship at the ziggurats, Mesopotamians had another way of keeping the gods happy—**astrology**! About 4,000 years ago, priests in Mesopotamia began using math to help them follow the movements of stars, planets, and the moon. If they saw bad **omens** in the night sky, they'd perform special rituals to try to stop any problems. They believed everything was written in the stars!

The world's oldest surviving horoscope is from Mesopotamia and is dated to April 29, 410 BCE.

WHAT DID THE STARS SAY?

THAT THE KING SHOULD BEWARE OF MIGHTY WINDS. WHAT COULD THAT MEAN?

HE SHOULD LAY OFF THE BEAN BURRITOS!

Stargazing priests tried to keep the gods happy so that the gods would protect the king. If the king was in danger, so was the whole kingdom!

The twelve astrological signs we recognize today come from the Mesopotamians.

Priests also looked at spots on the livers of sacrificed animals to figure out what the gods wanted. Gross!

The Mesopotamians created the first 12-month calendar based on the moon's phases.

Gods Gone Wild

Stargazing, worshipping, and offering sacrifices were all designed to please the Mesopotamian gods in order to avoid bad fortune. The many gods of Mesopotamia were an interesting bunch! Mesopotamian gods acted like humans. Sometimes they were good—and sometimes they were very bad. But they were never, ever boring!

Shamash was the god of the sun, justice, and law. People believed he **brought the sun across the sky each day in his chariot.**

CAN'T I EVER TAKE A DAY OFF?

IT'S TIME TO GO TO WORK, SHAMASH.

LET IT RIP, LEO!

CAN I ROAR NOW?

Ishtar, the goddess of love and war, also brought rain and thunderstorms. She was often shown with a lion whose roar was like thunder!

HEY, IT'S MY TURN, NOT YOURS! RRRROAR!!!

Nergal was an evil god of the **underworld** who brought **famine** and war.

Enlil was the god of air, wind, and storms. People also believed he controlled their fates—so they wanted to stay on his good side!

The god Enki was the shaper of the world and made plants grow. He is said to have **invented the plow.**

21

At Home in Mesopotamia

Keeping the moody gods happy was an important part of life in Mesopotamia, so there were lots of trips to the ziggurats. For this reason, homes were built near the temples. The houses were made of mud bricks that stayed cool in the summer and warm in the winter. Most houses had flat roofs where people slept outside in hot weather. People returned to their homes at night to enjoy family meals and evening entertainment.

While most people lived in simple mud brick houses, **kings lived in beautiful palaces with fancy decorations and sculptures.**

DON'T FORGET, WE HAVE A GIG AT THE PALACE THIS EVENING!

GREAT! FREE FOOD AND GOOD TIPS!

Wealthy Mesopotamians often paid musicians and singers to entertain them during meals. A little dinner music!

The Mesopotamians invented the world's oldest known board game. They first played the Royal Game of Ur more than 4,500 years ago!

AFTER 4,500 YEARS, I THINK WE'RE MISSING A FEW PIECES. . . .

Cuneiform tablets explaining the rules of the Royal Game of Ur have survived into the modern era. The game is still played today!

A typical Mesopotamian meal included bread, onions, and beer, along with fruits and vegetables. Meat was served on special occasions.

BOTTOMS UP!

I'LL TRADE YOU THIS ORANGE FOR A HAMBURGER.

WE DON'T HAVE MEAT HERE, KID. BUT WOULD YOU LIKE MY BRUSSELS SPROUTS?

WHAT A BUNCH OF SLOBS!

The Persian Empire

With their advanced math, huge cities, and mighty armies, the Mesopotamians were a force to be reckoned with. But one man decided he was up for the challenge. Cyrus the Great of Persia (now Iran) set his sights on Babylonia. Around 540 BCE, he attacked and defeated the Babylonian army and took control of the city of Babylon. He soon ruled all of Mesopotamia, which then became part of the Persian Empire—the largest empire on the world had ever seen!

After conquering Babylon, **Cyrus the Great freed 40,000 who had been enslaved and held prisoner there.**

YOU'RE WELCOME!

YOU'RE GREAT!

The Persian Empire stretched over 3,000 miles (4,828 km)— about the distance from New York City to Los Angeles!

The Persian king Xerxes I watched the Battle of Thermopylae from his seat on a golden throne carried by his soldiers. Sweet ride!

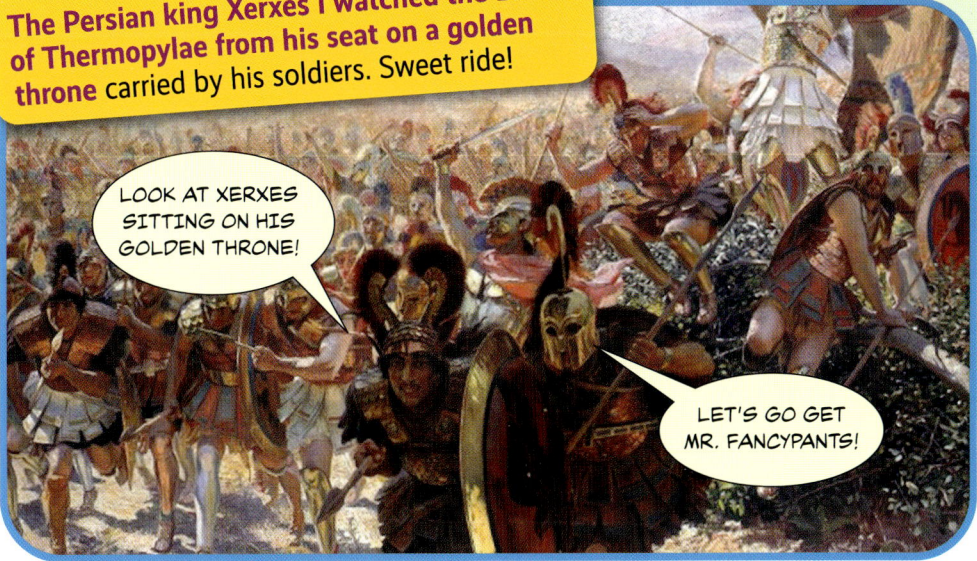

LOOK AT XERXES SITTING ON HIS GOLDEN THRONE!

LET'S GO GET MR. FANCYPANTS!

At the Battle of Thermopylae, Persia's army of 300,000 men took three days to defeat a Greek army of just 7,000 men.

The Persian Empire was finally conquered by Alexander the Great in 334 BCE. Nothing lasts forever!

Persians were the first to throw birthday parties, complete with cakes and birthday candles!

IS THAT GLUTEN FREE?

BIRTHDAY PARTIES ARE GREAT!

THANK YOU, PERSIANS!

Magnificent Mesopotamia

Mesopotamia didn't just give the world its very first civilization—it gave us basic things that we still use every day. Without the invention of the wheel, how would we move from place to place? Without a writing system, how would we communicate? And without laws, life would get really wild pretty fast! Let's take a look at some of Mesopotamia's other incredible inventions!

Mesopotamians invented soap almost 5,000 years ago! It was made from animal fat and wood ash. Such a fresh scent!

The earliest map was made in Mesopotamia about 4,300 years ago.

WHAT IS THIS MONSTROSITY?

IT'S THE MODERN VERSION OF YOUR PLOW!

The Mesopotamian invention of the plow led to the beginning of farming.

The first dog collar and leash were invented in Mesopotamia.

CONGRATULATIONS! YOU ARE THE FIRST DOG TO EVER WEAR A LEASH.

ARF! WORST . . . INVENTION . . . EVER!

The first toilet was invented 4,500 years ago! It was a brick seat built over a pit.

WHAT!? I'VE BUILT THE PERFECT REPLICA OF THE FIRST-EVER TOILET!

DOES THIS THING EVEN FLUSH?

Signatory Seals
Craft Project

In Mesopotamia, whenever you wanted to sign your name, you would take your personal seal and press it into a wet clay tablet. People often put their seals on strings and wore them like necklaces. Why not create your own seal and use it to sign something? Make your mark!

What You Will Need

- Air-dry clay
- Toothpicks
- Modeling clay
- Yarn
- Scissors

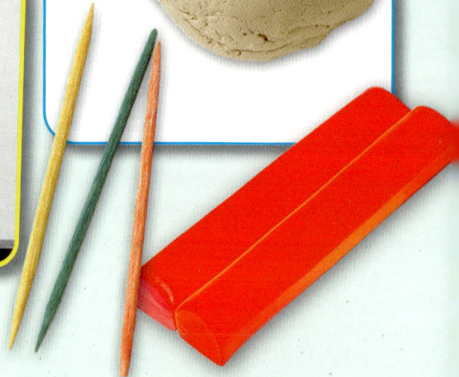

Ancient Mesopotamian seals and their impressions are displayed in museums.

Step One

Roll a small ball of air-dry clay. Flatten the ball into a thick pancake shape.

Step Two

Use a toothpick to draw the shape you want for your seal into the air-dry clay. Then, make a hole near the edge. Leave the clay to dry. This will become your seal.

Step Three

Next, try out signing with your seal. To do this, start by rolling out and flattening a piece of modeling clay. Then, place the modeling clay on a firm surface. Press your seal face down into the modeling clay.

Step Four

Carefully remove the seal from the modeling clay. Your mark will be left on the modeling clay.

Step Five

Finally, get ready to take your seal everywhere you go. Cut a piece of yarn long enough to fit over your head. Put it through the hole in the seal. Tie the two ends of the yarn together. Your seal necklace is finished.

29

Glossary

archaeologists scientists who learn about ancient times by studying things they dig up, such as old buildings, tools, and pottery

astrology the study of the influence that the stars and planets may have on people's lives

chariots horse-drawn vehicles with two wheels used in ancient times

complex a group of related things usually found together

crescent a curved shape that is wide in the center and pointed at the ends like a crescent moon

empire a large group of territories or people governed by one ruler

famine a time when there is a shortage of food

legends stories told from long ago

Middle East an area made up of several countries, including Iraq and Saudi Arabia, that covers parts of Asia and Africa

nomadic roaming or wandering from place to place

omens signs or warnings that seem to point to good or bad events in the future

rituals special ceremonies for religious or other purposes

sacrifices people or animals killed as part of a ceremony or as an offering to a god

underworld the place where some people believe that dead people go

wedge a piece of material shaped like a triangle with a thin edge

worship the act of honoring a god

Read More

Faust, Daniel R. *Ancient Mesopotamia (A Look at Ancient Civilizations).* New York: Gareth Stevens Publishing, 2019.

Green, Sara. *Ancient Mesopotamia (Blastoff! Discovery: Ancient Civilizations).* Minneapolis: Bellwether Media, 2020.

Nardo, Don. *Ancient Mesopotamia (Civilizations of the World).* Lake Elmo, MN: Focus Readers, 2020.

Learn More Online

1. Go to **www.factsurfer.com**

2. Enter "**Mesopotamia**" into the search box.

3. Click on the cover of this book to see a list of websites.

Index

Akkadians 7, 10

Ashurbanipal 15

Assyrians 10, 14–15

astrology 18, 24

Babylonians 10, 12, 14, 24, 27

Code of Hammurabi 12–13, 15

cuneiform 8–10, 15, 23

Cyrus the Great 24

Euphrates River 4, 6, 10

Fertile Crescent 4

Gilgamesh 4, 9, 15

gods 9, 11–12, 16–22

Hammurabi 10–15

Ishtar 20

Marduk 16

Persian Empire 24–25

priests 16–19

Shamash 12, 20

Sumerians 7–9, 16

Tigris River 4, 6

ziggurats 16–18, 22

About the Author

Catherine C. Finan is a writer living in northeastern Pennsylvania. She enjoys writing about a wide range of subjects, including ancient history. She'd like to thank the Mesopotamians for inventing the first toilet!